in God's World

Retreat Days for Older Primary Pupils

Simon Cocksedge
Priest-in-Charge, Edale, Derbyshire

Margaret Jones
Retired Parish Priest

GROVE BOOKS LIMITED
RIDLEY HALL RD CAMBRIDGE CB3 9HU

Contents

Acknowledgments

We are very grateful to the team at St Werburgh's Church of England Primary School, Spondon, who inspired the retreat days described here. We thank Sarah Tennant and Ben Acty, respectively former and current Wardens of the Peak Centre in Edale, Derbyshire, for their significant contributions to this work. We are also grateful for help and support from Sam Bradbury, Lesley Ayers and Chris Fisher at the Peak Centre, and Alison Brown and Alistair Langton at the Diocese of Derby.

AADE

Anglican Association of Directors of Education

First Impression April 2021

ISSN 2041-0964

ISBN 978 1 78827 159 2

1

Going on Retreat

The Peak Centre in Edale, Derbyshire, is a Christian youth residential centre linked with the Diocese of Derby. When a church primary school planning a residential for their Year 6 pupils included retreat time, the authors and Sarah Tennant—then Warden of the Peak Centre—were prompted to create a one-day retreat for local schools. Supported by the Diocese of Derby, these one-day retreats have been offered to Year 6 primary school children throughout Derbyshire every year since 2016. The authors have also run these retreat days in other venues and have given support/training to those wanting to offer retreat days to schools in their own locality.

This book presents our approach to these retreat days, including their theological and educational underpinning, along with relevant feedback from pupils and teachers. We hope that it will inspire readers to consider similar ventures elsewhere. Our tutor notes are available free online.[1]

What is a Retreat and Why Go on One?

The call of Jesus to 'come away and rest a while' has often been seen as the first invitation to make a retreat (Mark 6.31). Tracing the history of retreats is not easy but they perhaps originate from the 'retreat of the whole church' for Lent noted at the Council of Nicaea in 325AD.[2] St Ignatius of Loyola's sixteenth-century introduction of formal retreats as part of the Catholic Reformation was very influential. In the Anglican tradition, retreats increased remarkably in the late nineteenth and twentieth centuries.

Retreats in contemporary Western culture vary tremendously: a day at a spa; a weekend of cossetting at a boutique hotel; a week or more in a former Jesuit seminary; a month or two in a remote Buddhist monastery. All carry the same generic label. Some are simply for rest and pampering. Some prioritize prayer and silence. Some have talks and discussions with a particular theme, such as a saint's teaching or environmental issues. Others feature particular activities such as art, walking or poetry as aids to reflection.[3]

What they all have in common is the opportunity of taking time out from everyday life. A chance to reflect, rethink, regroup, refocus and re-energize. Space to step aside from life for a while, slow down and rest in a nurturing environment.

For many people, retreats are solely for physical and mental refreshment. For others, there is a spiritual context, such as seeking development or renewal in their relationship with God, and searching to quench the thirst deep in their 'non-physical selves':[4]

> Jesus often taught that the things of most value are not lying around on the surface of life. Like that hint of something buried in a field, there are hints and clues everywhere. But we must be willing to be distracted. We must break our routine, be inconvenienced and go out and buy a spade. (Matt 13.44)[5]

Why a Retreat for Year 6 Pupils?

We have found that there are several reasons why offering retreat days to children in Year 6 works well. As teachers readily affirm, this is a busy and often stressful year for pupils as they undertake their SATS and prepare to move on to secondary education. A retreat day offers them the chance to step away for a short while from the pressures they face, providing time to reflect on themselves and on their relationships with others, including with God. It is a welcome break for pupils and teachers alike.

Developmentally, at age 10 or 11 years, pupils are towards the end of childhood but they have not yet entered adolescence. This means their thinking is sufficient to obtain significant benefit through self-reflection (see chapter two for a fuller discussion on this point). By Year 6, children also tend to know each other reasonably well, which helps interactions during group activities.

Set within a Christian context, the day incorporates certain National Curriculum areas for Key Stage 2, helping to enhance what it is possible to deliver during the normal school day. These areas include Religious Education, PSHE (Personal, Social, Health Education), English, Citizenship and Music (see chapter six for more detail).

What Are the Aims of the Day?

Within a Christian context, pupils on this day are encouraged to:

- Look in at themselves.
- Look out at the world and others.
- Consider 'Who am I as a spiritual being?'

Key questions are:

- Who am I and why am I special?

- How do I listen to and talk with God?
- How do I respond to others?

Who is Involved?

The Year 6 retreat days that we offer are for one class (up to about 35 children). If schools have small classes, we often have two or occasionally three groups from different schools on the same day, which works well. The days need three tutors in the morning and two in the afternoon, in addition to staff accompanying their pupils. The programme for the day is the same for church and non-church schools (see chapter six).

How is the Day Structured?

Our experience suggests the following is a helpful way of structuring a retreat day:

- Opening plenary introducing the day.
- Working in three groups, pupils participate in a carousel of activities exploring:
  - ◊ Being a unique and special individual;
  - ◊ Learning to relax peacefully; and
  - ◊ Problem-solving and working together as a team.
- A brief plenary review of learning so far precedes lunch.
- After lunch, the topic of prayer is introduced and pupils then work in twos or threes at various prayer activity stations.

Learning from the whole day is shared at a closing plenary, followed by a brief time of worship. These activities, along with other aspects of the retreat day, are discussed in the chapters that follow. We also include feedback from both teachers and pupils, to help readers understand the different ways in which the retreat days have made an impact on all who participate.

2 Being Unique and Special

'Thank you for letting me find out why I am amazing.' (Lily-May, one week after retreat day)

'What I learned from the day was to realize who I was.' (Alia, one week after retreat day)

'The exercise enabled the students to think / reflect upon themselves but also to learn more about their peers.' (Teacher, at the end of retreat day)

Everyone is Unique and Valued

Throughout the New Testament, the teaching of Jesus, and then that of Paul and others, is that every person is unique, special and loved by God, whose love is overwhelming. However worthless, inadequate or far from anything spiritual we feel ourselves to be, we are loved, and whenever we turn towards God, that love is waiting for us:

> Are not five sparrows sold for two pennies? Yet not one of them is forgotten in God's sight. But even the hairs of your head are all counted. Do not be afraid; you are of more value than many sparrows. (Luke 12.6–7)

The aim of the Being Unique and Special session is to encourage each child to explore their sense of identity and worth, while naming the wider context of the love of God for each person and all creation. The focus of this activity is a button exercise which, while superficially simple, engages pupils straight away and can open teachers' eyes to previously unknown aspects of their pupils.

Session Outline: Being Unique and Special (30 mins)

- After a brief introduction explaining that, although we are all different, God has a loving plan for us all, pupils sit silently in a circle on the floor and think about all the things that make them special (sports, home, pets, school etc).
- A collection of buttons (all different) is spread out in the centre of the circle. In silence, children choose a button that reminds them of something, someone or somewhere special (*eg* a turquoise button for swimming or a special holiday).

- Each child explains why they chose their button, how it is distinctive and why they chose it from all the others. The leader prompts further exploration: *eg* 'Why is it so special when you walk your dog?' 'How does it feel?'
- In silence, children draw something relating to what they have described. This work is taken back to school for completion or discussion.
- To close, each child shares one or two words that have arisen for them during this activity. The leader reiterates God's love for every unique person.

The Development of Children's Understanding

Madeleine Simon, an experienced teacher of Christianity and prayer to children, describes the way a child's understanding of God develops.[6] She suggests it starts for under-sevens through straightforward storytelling, so that they begin a personal relationship with Jesus. Seven to nine year-olds take part in the storytelling through activities, so they move 'towards an experienced understanding that love calls for a response of love.' By Years 5 and 6, she regards children as able to realize that the parables, such as the Lost Sheep or the Woman's Lost Coin, demonstrate the uniqueness of each person in God's eyes and God's love for each and every one.

While Simon acknowledges that her age categories are not fixed, since children mature at different rates, she captures something of the changes in children's understanding as their personalities develop. In Erik Erikson's theory of personality development, Year 5 and 6 pupils are nearing the end of childhood, which precedes adolescence.[7] At this age, in a stage called 'Industry (competence) *v* Inferiority,' many new skills are being learnt. Although some failure is necessary for learning and growth, failing to acquire these skills, or to keep up with peers, can result in feelings of inferiority, which may be long lasting and can inhibit attainment of full potential. These feelings will be exacerbated without appropriate encouragement from adults and teachers.

Success in this stage, according to Erikson, leads to competence. Failure, on the other hand, may have ongoing impact on feelings of worth and personality development. There are many theories around personality development but this example demonstrates the importance of valuing and encouraging each child in their unique path to maturity. This is significant both for individuals and for society.

Encouraging Well-being

The subjective well-being of children is always a concern for parents and professionals alike.[8] In a class of thirty, there are likely to be several children with significantly low well-being; at the time of writing, during the COVID-19 pandemic, this is a particular worry, especially as it can link with mental health conditions such as anxiety and depression.[9] Our experience is that, while surprises do sometimes emerge during this activity, such as a recent bereavement or a loss from the past that remains currently important, teachers are generally aware of these issues in their children. Additionally, if such issues do arise for a child, their peers in the group are usually supportive.

In *A PSHE and Wellbeing Framework for Primary Schools*, the Health Education Partnership identifies that Year 6 pupils need to learn to recognize the contribution that their individuality and personal qualities make to their mental health and well-being.[10] Any activity which affirms children's self-worth should encourage their feelings of well-being.

In this button exercise, exploration of a child's uniqueness enables a positive experience, valuing each contribution made to the group and allowing children to learn from their peers. Participants touch on their sense of worth in a supportive atmosphere, which is very different from the everyday pressures of school classes and SATS. This uniqueness is then reinforced through drawing. Children regularly contextualize their uniqueness in terms of their family and the wider community, along with hobbies such as sport and music.

> 'Although I am unique, I'm also part of a community, a school, a family, and I'm a sister, a daughter, a carer.' (Katie, one week after retreat day)
>
> 'This session gave staff a greater insight into pupils and their beliefs.' (Two teachers, one year after retreat day)

The emphasis in this button activity is on self-worth and uniqueness. God's love for every person, irrespective of how they feel, is a fundamental Christian belief, which we ask facilitators to mention at the beginning—and towards the end—of this session. This balance of emphasis is, in part, so that the first half of the day focuses on each child as an individual, and the second on Christian prayer and their response to it. Also, in a busy day like this, it is only possible to touch on aspects of faith and individual religious beliefs. Nevertheless, feedback suggests the children still hear this message clearly on the day and remember it several months later:

> 'I learned that I am special because I am unique, and different from everybody else. I also took from the day that I am a child of God. No

matter what I do, or who I am, God will always love me.' (Evie, one week after retreat day)

'I learnt that I am unique and different to everybody in the class. I also learned that I am a child of God.' (Fred, fourteen weeks after retreat day)

3 Time to De-stress

'Today I've learnt how when I get angry there's a way I can relax.' (Josh, during the day's closing plenary)

'The drawing activity we did when we picture our special place in our minds calms me down and comforts me when I am lost, upset or stressed or just need some time on my own.' (Megan, six months after retreat day)

'One of the most valuable parts of the day, from the children's point of view, was the opportunity to experience meditation and relaxation techniques. It was not surprising how much they valued the stillness, calm and quiet, which often play very little part in their day to day lives. "Why don't we do this more?" was their common response.' (Form teacher, two weeks after retreat day)

The Need for Stillness

The modern world is a stressful place in which to live and the majority of children are not exempt from pressure of one sort or another. It is also a very noisy place and one in which our minds are constantly bombarded with stimuli, including the non-stop intrusion of technology and social media. Noel Keating suggests, 'There is an urgent need for silence and stillness in the modern world,' but children, seeing how adults behave, 'become conditioned to think that this is how life must be…[which] inhibits their innate understanding of the need for stillness and silence.'[11]

One of the carousel of activities that we offer during these retreat days is a guided visualization. This provides an opportunity to begin to develop some of the skills needed in our stressful, noisy world, skills that the Health Education Partnership identifies as important for the mental health and well-being of Year 6 pupils.[12] The activity encourages the children to be still and silent. They then take part in a guided visualization, which is a relaxation technique that draws on an ability to use the imagination to visualize a peaceful scene. This visualization is enhanced by using all the senses which encourages the children not just to think about what they are seeing, hearing, feeling, smelling and tasting but also to experience it as if they are actually present.

This might be a new experience for some children, but since an increasing number of schools now teach mindfulness, habits of the mind and / or growth mindset, other pupils on the retreat day will have encountered this technique.

Session Outline:
Time to De-stress—Guided Visualization (30 mins)

- A setting is needed that is spacious enough for children to sit or lie comfortably (beanbags and / or cushions are ideal but not essential).
- A brief introduction includes the aims, which are:
  - ◊ To teach the children a relaxation technique; and
  - ◊ To encourage them to use their imaginations to create, in their minds, a safe space to which they can retreat.
- After a short relaxation exercise, the children are led through a guided visualization, encouraging them to use their imaginations and their senses.
- At the end of the visualization, the leader asks the children to leave their imaginary place and, when ready, to open their eyes and sit up.
- Before any discussion, the children record something from their visualization. This may be a drawing, a poem or simply a series of words.
- The children are encouraged to talk about the activity, sharing how easy or difficult they found the exercise and explaining things they saw and heard etc.
- At the end, the leader explains that the place they have been imagining is somewhere safe and special, and somewhere they can return to whenever they wish to still their minds and relax.

Being intentionally still and silent are vital elements of this guided visualization and, as such, identify this as a form of meditation. There is evidence that meditating regularly—whether from a secular, religious or spiritual perspective—has a significant role to play in 'enhancing human performance and maintaining good health and well-being.'[13] This includes 'a heightened sense of emotional well-being, enhanced openness, and improved self-esteem.'[14] As the created scene unfolds through the guided visualization, 'the imagination projects into our conscious mind thoughts, memories and feelings which, although hidden from us in our subconscious, are, in fact, influencing our perception, thinking and acting.'[15]

Focusing attention on images as part of the visualization 'helps to quieten the self-conscious mind,' and 'gives rise to a sense of calm, peace and balance that benefits both overall health and emotional well-being.' The silence whilst meditating is also important for the human psyche because it 'is like a circuit breaker—it breaks the incessant pattern of unrelenting stimuli and noise. It reduces both internal and external "noise" and stress and restores us to harmony.'[16] It has also been identified as an effective method for building resilience.[17]

> 'I learnt a lot about how to relax and to realize that I can make my own safe space anywhere and can go to it when I'm feeling stressed.' (Kyle, five months after retreat day)
>
> 'I learnt that God wants us to live a happy life by being relaxed more and not stressed by things.' (Millie, six months after retreat day)
>
> 'The children enjoyed the meditation and I have [since led] another meditation session where the children were encouraged to relax in the safe space they have imagined.' (Teacher, fourteen weeks after retreat day)

Imagination and Meditation

Children find the experience of meditation enjoyable, not least because it is non-competitive, not measured and not tested. The only thing that is required of them is 'the intention simply to be.'[18] Madeline Simon suggests that children, in fact, have a natural contemplative gift and thus the practice of meditation comes naturally to them.[19] This is supported by research from the World Community of Christian Meditation (WCCM)[20] that children like to meditate and often choose to meditate at home following experience in the classroom, suggesting the transfer of classroom skills into everyday life. Additionally, the consensus of teachers who use meditation as a regular practice with their pupils, is that this life skill is important and beneficial from a mental health perspective to individual children while also contributing to school life, altering attitudes and class atmosphere.[21]

Imagination, an important part of any visualization, has a long history in prayer and contemplation in Christian tradition. Perhaps the best documented example is in St Ignatius of Loyola's *Spiritual Exercises* from the sixteenth century. 'Imagination played a central role in [Loyola's] conversion…he discovered how useful the imagination could be in fostering a deeper relationship with God.'[22]

The visualization the children engage with on this occasion is a form of meditation. Although set within the Christian context of our retreat days, this is a generic exercise with no religious focus. Children's responses to the experience suggest that it helps them to feel happier, more peaceful and more grateful for the good things in life. For some children this activity may become a spiritual experience. Rebecca Nye identifies children's spiritual experience as a 'relational consciousness,' suggesting that they have an innate capacity for forming relationships, not only with themselves but also with others, including with creation and with God.[23]

As many schools today are multi-faith, multi-ethnic and multicultural, the appropriateness of using meditation, whether secular or spiritual, may be questioned. However, most researchers in this field acknowledge that meditation is common ground for all wisdom traditions, a powerful and potentially transformative shared meeting point where words and symbols temporarily give way to silence:

> It is the common understanding of the wisdom and religion traditions that meditation promotes greater self-awareness, individual and communal well-being, and human flourishing.[24]

Whilst retreat days such as we are describing are clearly set in a Christian context, our experience is that children of other faiths and of none engage fully with this and all the activities.

4 Working with Others

'Today I've learnt that if we're to work as a team, it's important to listen to each other.' (Jason, at the end of the retreat day)

'I found it interesting to see different children coming to the fore during the team-building activities, rather diffidently at first.' (Teacher, fourteen weeks after retreat day)

Two questions raised during these retreat days are *Who am I?* and *How do I respond to others?* These questions recognize the importance of children being enabled to build their sense of identity and belonging, and to develop a respect for others. One of the morning carousel of activities, the session on problem solving and working together is one way in which children can address these questions. The activities encourage thinking about the skills needed to work well as a team and about interactions with one another, such as being able to communicate well and actively listen.

Session Outline: Working with Others (30 mins)

Magic Stick

- Working in a group of between six and eight, children stand in two lines facing each other and pointing the index finger of each hand out in front of them.
- A cane is balanced on their outstretched index fingers; they are told the aim is to lower the stick to the ground without holding on to it.
- At first, the stick will go up or become lopsided. They try again.
- The leader stops the activity and asks the children to reflect on what is happening, why they cannot achieve the objective and how they could work better together.
- They try again, hopefully successfully.

Dragon Design

- Working in a group of between six and eight, the children's task is to make themselves corporately into a dragon or monster, with one end as head, the other as tail.

- Rules: the only contact the dragon / monster can have with the floor is one head, two bottoms, one back, four feet, four hands.
- The leader sets a time limit and reminds them of this at intervals.
- The leader counts down at the end of the time so that the children can get themselves into the shape.
- Everyone discusses what worked / did not work, and reflects on the skills or qualities that are important if a team is to work together successfully.

During and at the conclusion of each activity, a discussion facilitated by the leader helps children to begin to reflect on and understand their interactions as team members. Christians believe that God created humans in his own image (Gen 1.27) and that everybody is unique, with unique abilities as well as natural strengths and weaknesses (Ps 139.13–15). Yet, although each person is unique, we are interdependent and, to use St Paul's analogy of the body, we need one another if the body is to be complete (1 Cor 12.14ff).

Team Players

The problem-solving engaged in during this session helps to develop skills taught in Key Stage 2 PSHE, including teamwork, valuing the different contributions that people make to the community, and pupils recognizing positive things about themselves and their achievements. Meredith Belbin, who has undertaken considerable research into teamwork, notes that in a successful team each team member usually has clear responsibilities. His observations of individual behaviours and interpersonal relationships have led him to define a team role as 'a tendency to behave, contribute and interrelate with others in a particular way.' He has identified nine specific team roles and contends that teams are most effective when they are balanced and consist of individuals able to contribute to these various behavioural areas. Belbin further maintains that if you understand your role in a team, it is possible to 'develop your strengths and manage your weaknesses as a team member, and so improve how you contribute to the team.'[25]

'Today I've learnt that if we're to work as a team it's important to listen to each other.' (Martha, at the end of retreat day)

'I learned that there isn't one leader in a group. Everyone is the leader because everyone needs to be heard and everyone needs to take part.' (Ryan, one week after retreat day)

'I've learnt that communication is key if you want to do well as a team.' (Elsie, one week after retreat day)

Ryan, who recognized that each member of a team needs to be heard and needs to take part if the team is to be effective, showed considerable astuteness. There is often an assumption that, in a particular situation, one person adopts a leadership role, but often, as Stephen Cottrell suggests, the more effective leader allows their leadership to be led.[26]

Listening and Leadership

In their discussion about these problem-solving activities, the children can recognize that listening attentively to 'the challenges of the situation they are in, and also to the views, advice and experience of those they are working with' is a key skill.[27] They can also begin to identify the leadership qualities that one or more of the group demonstrates, and to recognize that the person who says most is not necessarily the one who helps them to achieve most. The more successful leader often builds consensus by involving everyone in the team. They show trust by valuing and developing each person's contribution and, because their goal is the success of the team, they are prepared to be followers too. In this way, 'Things get done. Everyone says they have done it themselves.'[28]

Once the exercises have been completed, it is important to encourage children to consider their own interactions with other group members. This allows reflection on what they have learned about themselves, as well as what they have learned about, and from, those with whom they have worked. This is particularly relevant since children will not necessarily have been in a group with those they usually work with at school.

'I enjoyed this activity because the group I was put into was with people I don't really spend time with, but we worked as a great team.' (Bella, at the end of the day)

At the end of Year 6, most children move on to a much larger school where they will find themselves working with children they do not know well. Hence the usefulness of emphasizing these teamwork and problem-solving skills.

5

Talking with God

'I like knowing the different ways to pray and talk to God.' (Alia, six months after retreat day)

'The retreat day offered the children an opportunity to pray and develop their understanding of prayer and its significance.' (Form teacher, six months after retreat day)

Prayer, which has been defined as conversing with, or relating to, God, has been recorded as part of religious activity since the earliest biblical accounts. Jesus prayed regularly and prayer has a long history as an integral component of Christian faith, although there is, of course, no Christian monopoly on prayer.[29] Prayer can also be confusing, as one teacher noted:

> Prayer, for children and adults, is a difficult concept to understand. How does God hear them? Does he hear? Why aren't they answered? Can God only hear a prayer if I say it aloud? With my hands together? In a special building? (Teacher, six months after retreat day)

Throughout our retreat days children are exposed to a variety of experiences of prayer, which address some of these questions. The aim is for pupils to learn something of what prayer is about in a Christian context and to have a go at praying, at putting it into action. In the afternoon session, we offer a very practical, highly experiential introduction to various ways of praying in the Christian tradition. We find that pupils, including those of different faiths and none, almost invariably respond enthusiastically to this.

The objective is to make children aware of various prayer tools. Some may be immediately useful; some they might use later; some they may never come across again; whilst some, teachers may pick up and reuse at school. Each tool can be traced back in Christian history (as we describe briefly below).

Session Outline: Talking with God (about 90 mins)

- *Introduction,* including:
  - ◊ Hearing the children's ideas about what prayer is; and

- ◊ Explaining ways of praying based on the ACTS mnemonic (adoration, contrition (forgiveness), thanksgiving, supplication [1 Tim 2.1]).

- *Prayer stations*—sixteen are listed in the tutor notes—we use at least twelve each time:
  - ◊ Children circulate round them in pairs or trios;
  - ◊ Each station involves an activity based on one or more of the ACTS ways of praying; and
  - ◊ Every child writes a short prayer and also decorates a stone to say thank you (for example for family, friends etc) which they take with them at the end of the day.
- *Prayer walk*—we walk in prayerful silence to the final plenary venue for a time of prayer together. Children are asked to listen and look and be thankful for the wonderful creation all around.
- *Prayer together* with sharing of experiences—a final plenary uses music and candles with the children sitting in a circle:
  - ◊ A cairn is built, with each child adding their own prayer stone, symbolizing their journey;
  - ◊ Everyone contributes something they learnt from the day; and
  - ◊ There is silence, singing, music and reading out of written prayers from the prayer stations, concluding with a closing prayer.

Learning to Pray Using Prayer Stations

Using prayer stations is a well-established method for helping people learn about a variety of ways of praying.[30] Stations can be stand-alone or use themes such as movement, art/creativity or rest. Our stations use the ACTS mnemonic. This simple tool emerges from St Paul's biblical phrase, 'I urge that supplications, prayers, intercessions, and thanksgivings should be made for everyone' (1 Tim 2.1).

These headings can also be seen within the Lord's Prayer, taught by Jesus, which gives a pattern for all Christian praying:

> 'Our Father'—we come before God with others.
> 'Hallowed be your name'—we give God thanks and praise.
> 'Your kingdom come, your will be done'—we look for God's will for us.
> 'Give us this day our daily bread'—we bring to God our needs.
> 'Forgive us our sins…'—we request forgiveness and that we too can be forgiving.
> 'Lead us not into temptation'—we ask for strength and protection.

Based on the ACTS headings, our stations involve experiencing prayer through active participation. To help children's understanding, we change the key words to: adoring, saying sorry / forgiveness, thanksgiving and asking God.

Examples include:

- Looking in a mirror at one's reflection, to encourage thankfulness for our unique selves.
- Blowing bubbles then watching them float away and burst, which provides a metaphor for saying sorry and receiving forgiveness.
- Looking at stones and gems in a clear bowl of still water, leading to prayers of praise about creation and asking forgiveness for its mistreatment by human beings.
- Viewing a world map laid on the floor and placing a marker on a country where there is war, poverty or other problems—this allows reflection on pain and sadness, which is then offered to God for healing.

Other Tools for Learning to Pray

In addition to prayer stations, children participate in other experiences of prayer throughout the retreat day and during the final plenary. All of these provide insight into prayer and the tools for praying.

Walking

At some venues, it is possible to take a walk outside and experience walking as prayer. Feeling the wind on one's cheeks, listening to the rustle of the leaves and the singing of the birds, looking at plants and trees, feeling our muscles stretching in the fresh air—becoming aware of these simple everyday sensations allows us to pause in our busyness and to give thanks for all creation around us. Such awareness-raising provides a simple tool for future prayer.[31]

Singing

The saying 'The one who sings prays twice' is attributed to St Augustine of Hippo (354–430AD). We explain this as meaning that, while we physically use our bodies to sing the words, we also pray them, thus both our bodies and our minds are praying. Using simple words repetitively is a well-known way of focusing one's mind in prayer. It can be traced back as far as the monks of the Egyptian desert in the fourth century. Often phrases from the Bible are used but, as Simon notes, other words work just as well.[32]

The group learn the repetitive song *Father we adore you* near the start of the day and this is repeated later. Towards the end of the day, they are asked to sing it from memory with their eyes shut and to offer the simple words as a prayer. We often hear reports that the bus back to school has been filled with this prayerful singing and that this has carried on subsequently. 'The song was awesome,' wrote one pupil in her thank-you letter.

Silence

Times of silence are built into the day. They are brief but significant, usually of no more than two to three minutes. Although the WCCM offer the guideline that children can cope with a minute of silence for each year of their age, it takes practice and we find many Year 6 schoolchildren are not used to using time in this way. Those that are often use it as part of mindfulness meditation.

Using silence in prayer has been well reported, beginning with the Bible and accounts from fourth-century Egypt.[33] Such silent contemplative prayer is often described as simply sitting before God, perhaps using a candle or some other symbol. Within a retreat day packed with activity, these brief spaces give children a taster of silence and often give staff confidence to try teaching and using silence in collective worship.

Place

At the beginning of the day, we introduce the idea of retreating away from all our usual activities to have some space and recharge our batteries. This is hard to do in a noisy school, hence the value of travelling to the day's venue. At the end of the day, we meet together for a time of sharing experiences and worship. We try to gather in a special place, such as the chancel or side chapel of the church or the hut amongst the trees at the Peak Centre. This enables a brief discussion of the importance of place both in praying and in having a retreat.

As the retreat day concludes, moving to a different location for the closing reflections and prayers allows us to mention that, while some places are special for prayer, prayer can be anywhere. Special places can feel different, often being described as thin spots or sacred spaces where the atmosphere or gap between earth and heaven is thinned. They can be enhanced by music, by images such as paintings or glass, and by candles or other lighting. A prayer corner in the classroom or home is part of this tradition, as is a church building.

Everyday Prayer

While prayer can involve silence, singing or special times or places, it is much more often just part of everyday living. We spontaneously pray for people we love or those who are sick, or we might offer thanks for a beautiful sunset or time with a friend. Some of the prayer stations (such as those involving playdough or writing a prayer) encourage these simple and direct 'quickie' or 'arrow' prayers.

Discussion and Impact

'One of the main things that I learnt was that there is more than one way of praying, like burning our mistakes. Also, the peaceful song that you led: we taught it to my cousin and now we sing it in the car together.' (Rebecca, seven months after retreat day)

'The retreat day practically supported pupils in the act of prayer, giving them new and appealing ways to talk to God—ideas that they are keen to share with others back in school. Indeed, the children produced "Practical Guides to Prayer" to display and share in school.' (Form teacher, one year after retreat day)

Prayer in schools can sometimes be problematic (although generally, not for the children who pray). The challenge in schools is to release and channel an innate spirituality into prayer and reflection, rather than to impose stilted prayers on unwilling hearts and minds.[34]

Most writers about children and prayer are clear that young people, particularly of primary-school age, are ready to engage and participate in prayer. Any reticence usually comes from adult organizers. If sessions are well prepared, carefully explained and not too long, children readily take part in praying and prayerful activities.

Feedback suggests that exploring and experiencing prayer during these retreat days works for pupils and teachers, both in the short and long term. Children like the independence of working in pairs or trios and the wide variety of the prayer stations. They also clearly become very comfortable with both singing and silence throughout the day.

Teachers almost invariably feed back that numerous curriculum areas are covered in the sections on prayer, including RE (specifically prayer and talking to God), Arts (creativity, music) and SMSC (Spiritual, Moral, Social and Cultural Development). They also take ideas away to use back at school, such as displays, presentations, children leading collective worship based on material from the retreat day, as well as a class of Year 6 pupils running their own retreat afternoon for a Year 1 class (see chapter six).

The message for teachers from this work is, first, to have confidence to explore prayer and children's spirituality. Your pupils will go with you and may go ahead of you! Secondly, there is no need to reinvent the wheel; plenty of helpful material is out there.

6 Retreat Day Impact

In this final chapter, we assess the impact of our retreat days in the hope of enthusing others who might wish to run similar days. Our analysis uses feedback we have received from teachers and pupils over five years, given to us at both the end of the day they attended and at intervals afterwards. This analysis is structured round the aims and key questions of the day (see chapter one).

Looking In at Ourselves: Who am I and Why am I Special?

Finding a quiet space to reflect on our lives is hard to achieve in the busyness of everyday life, let alone during the average school day. Many teachers and pupils spoke of the value of simply having a day away from the classroom and appreciated its clear focus and very different structure. Significantly, even months after the retreat day, they still remembered the importance of taking this time out.

> 'It helped you to think about who you are.' (Amy, seven months after retreat day)
>
> 'Most useful was the time for children to be still and reflect about their lives. They really appreciated the time out message of the day. This is something we forget to do in our busy lives.' (Teacher, at end of retreat day)
>
> 'The retreat provides a day of reflection—important in the busy lives of today's children. It equips children with ways to relax, reflect and think deeply about matters, providing strategies that enable them to take time out of the stresses of modern life, whilst offering them ways to make their own sense of matters, as they learn to reflect independently.' (Teacher, seven months after retreat day)
>
> 'Children's feedback, in discussion following the retreat day, was enthusiastic. Developmentally, the vast majority of Year 6 children are beyond the egocentric stage and are very open to asking questions about their place in the world. The morning activities allowed the children to focus on themselves and to be calm, still and centred in a way that they wouldn't normally do.' (Teacher, five months after retreat day)

In all the feedback we have received, there has never been a negative comment about spending time together in silence or about reflection on the self. Children are ready to participate and, as discussed in chapter two, by the age of 10 or 11 years, they are able to be reflective and to look at and question themselves and their world.

Looking Out at the World and Responding to Others

As discussed in chapter four, the problem-solving and teamwork activities undertaken during the day help children to reflect on, and learn more about, themselves and the ways in which they need to relate to one another if they are to attain successful outcomes. These include listening, communication and leadership skills.

Some of the prayer station activities also encourage children to focus on the wider world and to consider their place in it. Their comments following the retreat day show the impact of this.

> 'I enjoyed working as a team together like when we were trying to make a monster using our bodies. I enjoyed doing them because it made me realize that to make things work, we need to work as a team and communicate.' (Holly, one day after retreat day)
>
> 'The best bit for me was doing the map activity: you needed to put a stone on a place that was suffering from something bad happening. I put mine on Antarctica, because they are suffering from global warming.' (James, one day after retreat day)
>
> 'On the way, we saw the clouds touch the top of the mountain and that was truly amazing! [At one prayer station] we were blowing bubbles which slowly fell down and, as they fell down, we reflected on the past and hoped for a better future.' (Albert, one day after retreat day)
>
> 'I think the world map activity was especially good because it helped us to think about things that are happening in the world.' (Edward, fourteen weeks after retreat day)

Who am I as a Spiritual Being?

Clarifying what it means to be a spiritual being is not easy. Spirituality has been defined as expressing:

> ...a sense that human life involves more than biology [and that] as human beings, we are naturally driven by goals beyond physical sat-

isfaction or mental supremacy to seek a deeper level of meaning and fulfilment.[35]

Thus, understanding ourselves as spiritual beings means recognizing the integration of life as a whole, linking the depths of ordinary human existence with searching for the meaning and purpose of life and the sacred. Taking a retreat day away from school may allow this search to begin, though our experience is that it is rarely explicitly named as spiritual.

'It has helped me to think deeper about things.' (Dane, seven months after retreat day)

'The Scrabble letters worked well because the activity made me think about what God is.' (Shahan, fourteen weeks after retreat day)

'As the prayer activities in the afternoon used different approaches—visual, auditory and kinaesthetic—they attracted different children in different ways. Again, in discussions, the one that most children responded to involved prayer stones. Some children felt very protective about "their" stone as it represented something that they weren't able to put into words.' (Teacher, five months after retreat day)

'It provided an opportunity for pupils to consider their spirituality and to understand they can be spiritual, even if they do not follow a religion.' (Two teachers, seven months after retreat day)

How Do I Listen to and Talk with God?

Prayer is part of how we search for the sacred in life. There is no right or wrong way to pray, so offering children a variety of approaches through a series of activities allows them to experience prayer as both something spiritual and also as something very tangible and doable.

'My favourite part was going round in partners and praying in lots of different ways. It was fascinating learning how many different ways you can pray.' (Beth, one week after retreat day)

'It was fun and one of the best days of my life—I learnt how to pray to God more often.' (Stephen, one week after retreat day)

'I really enjoyed when we put one of the sins that we have previously committed on paper, then ripped it up. We then put it in the fire, to symbolize how easily God would forgive us for doing the sin.' (Michael, one day after retreat day)

This may be easier for children to absorb than for those responsible for their education.

> 'The [flyer] suggested a lot of prayer and we were concerned that this might put children off. However, the reality was more balanced and also gave the teacher ideas to use back at school.' (Head teacher, one week after retreat day)

To be authentic, we make it clear that anything said about spirituality and prayer on these retreat days comes from a Christian context. An example would be an introduction that included: 'As Christians, this is what we as your retreat leaders believe. Not everyone believes the same things and we all need to be respectful of each other's belief systems.'

How Does this Day Contribute to the School Curriculum?

Teachers almost invariably acknowledge the wide curriculum content covered on these retreat days, including PSHE, RE, English (see box for more detail), Music (singing in a round) and Physical Education (teamwork). Other areas of the curriculum sometimes noted are Arts (creativity), SMSC (Spiritual, Moral, Social and Cultural Development) and Citizenship (thinking of how community works; contemplating impact of belief on actions).

Details of Curriculum Areas Covered in RE, PSHE and English

- *RE:* Purpose of prayer; talking to God through praying; forgiveness; spiritual and moral topics; Christianity; worship.
- *PHSE:* mental well-being; cooperation; teamwork; community; global links; relaxation and calming; appreciating others; how am I special?; self-belief, self-worth, self-acceptance; social skills; diversity; respecting others; knowing our own and others' strengths and weaknesses.
- *English:* speaking, listening, responding, explaining ideas; creative / imaginative writing; literacy.

Comments from teachers also identify that the day tackles areas that can be hard to cover in school. For example, one teacher at the end of a day noted the importance of 'the focus on well-being and range of activities to engage and broaden and address areas perhaps not always given enough time in today's busy curriculum: also some time to "stand and stare," to think about the world and realize awe and wonder.' Two other teachers, seven months after the retreat day, noted that it 'provided a "church" focus—supporting our Christian distinctiveness.'

Examples of Further Development of Retreat Day Material Back at School

There is much from the day that can be taken back to school and reused.

> 'Even better, as any school teacher will heartily affirm, [activities] were easy to pick up and take back to school with us. Stones, bubbles, lolly-sticks, playdough, buttons, sticky notes, beanbags, bamboo canes and pencils all helped the children to experience imaginative ways to pray and reflect.' (Teacher, two weeks after retreat day)
>
> 'Having been asked how we could make some of these ideas and activities accessible to much younger children, the Year 6 pupils led a similar set of activities the following week, as a Year 1 afternoon retreat.' (Teacher, fourteen weeks after retreat day)
>
> 'The children produced "Practical Guides to Prayer" to display and share in school.' (Teacher, one year after retreat day)

Teachers are frequently surprised, but appreciative, of the fact that they learn new things about some of their pupils. For instance, this may come during teamwork activities, in which unexpected leadership skills often emerge. It may also come during the button activity when children sometimes reveal significant information, such as concern about a sick but much-loved relative or pet.

Similarly, pupils also frequently report learning new things about their peers, which helps them in thinking about how they respond to others (one of the day's key questions).

> 'At Edale, we learnt that each one of us is special and different in our own way and that we don't have to work with our friends all the time and that we can enjoy working with other people instead.' (Eliza, one week after retreat day)

Our experience is that this day is equally helpful for both church and non-church schools, and for children of all faiths and none. No changes are made to either advertising or content when delivering this day to non-church schools. Tutors are trained always to carefully phrase and contextualize the

Christian basis of this day irrespective of which school(s) is participating (see previous section).

Lastly, teachers often experience the day as a retreat or time out for themselves, one reflecting, 'I loved the day—it was as useful to me as it was for the children.'

Conclusion

We were nervous about setting up these retreat days. Would any school be prepared to give up a day to something so apparently esoteric? Could we engage the children for a whole day? Would the response be positive?

'Yes' is the answer to all these questions. We hope this book portrays our enthusiasm about holding retreat days for older primary pupils and encourages you to think about organizing a similar day in your context. Our ambition is that a retreat day like this is offered at every school (church or non-church) throughout Derbyshire and beyond. Our tutor notes provide detailed information about setting up and running a retreat day and are freely available for you to use.[36]

> 'I would thoroughly recommend this special and memorable day to other primary schools across the Diocese of the Derby. Our children are willing, ready and very likely to exceed our expectations when given a chance to experience all this in such a beautiful environment!' (Teacher, two weeks after retreat day)

Notes

1 For tutor notes for primary school retreat days, see: https://www.peakcentre.org.uk/pdfs/Primary%20Retreat%20Days%20TUTOR%20NOTES.pdf If you need support or training, please contact us by email via the Peak Centre—details on website: www.peakcentre.org.uk

2 A Luther, 'Retreats,' in P Sheldrake (ed), *The New SCM Dictionary of Christian Spirituality* (London: SCM Press, 2005) p 541.

3 For more information on retreats, try the Retreat Association: http://www.retreats.org.uk/index.php or the Association for Promoting Retreats: http://www.promotingretreats.org/why-go-on-a-retreat/

4 B Holt, *A Brief History of Christian Spirituality* (Oxford: Lion, 2003) p 11.

5 D Runcorn, *Spirituality Workbook: A Guide for Explorers, Pilgrims and Seekers* (London: SPCK, 2006) p 2.

6 M Simon, *Born Contemplative: Introducing Children to Christian Meditation* (London: Medio Media, 2010) pp 77–88.

7 E Phares and W Chaplin, *Introduction to Personality* (Lebanon, IN: Prentice Hall, fourth edition, 1997) p 118.

8 The Childrens' Society, 'The Good Childhood Report 2019' (accessed 10 August 2020, https://www.childrenssociety.org.uk/what-we-do/resources-and-publications/the-good-childhood-report-2019)

9 The Children's Society, 'Life on Hold: Children's Well-being and COVID-19,' July 2020 (Accessed 10 August 20: https://www.childrenssociety.org.uk/sites/default/files/life-on-hold-childrens-well-being-and-covid-19.pdf).
10 The Health Education Partnership, 'A PSHE and Well-being Framework for Primary Schools,' 2017 (accessed July 2020: https://www.healtheducationpartnership.com/resources/Tri-B_PSHE_Framework_Primary.pdf) p 33.
11 N Keating, *Meditation with Children—A Resource for Teachers and Parents* (Dublin: Veritas, 2017) pp 21–22.
12 The Health Education Partnership, *op cit,* p 33.
13 S Nataraja, *The Blissful Brain: Neuroscience and Proof of the Power of Meditation* (London: Octopus, 2008) p 14.
14 Keating, *op cit,* p 28.
15 A Solomon, *Praying with Imagination* (2019). Retrieved from: https://www.spiritual-life.co.uk/single-post/2016/06/05/Praying-with-the-Imagination
16 Keating, *op cit,* p 22–26.
17 M Greenberg and A Harris, 'Nurturing Mindfulness in Children and Youth: Current State of Research' in *Child Development Perspectives* (June 2012) pp 1–6, DOI: 10.1111/j.1750-8606.2011.00215.x
18 Keating, *op cit,* p 93.
19 Simon, *op cit,* p 2.
20 The World Community for Christian Meditation; https://wccm.org/teaching-resources/meditation-with-children (accessed May 2021).
21 Keating, *op cit,* p 207.
22 D Fleming, *What is Ignatian Spirituality?* (Chicago, IL: Loyola Press, 2008) p 55.
23 R Nye, *Children's Spirituality: What It Is and Why It Matters* (London: Church House Publishing, 2009).
24 Keating, *op cit,* p 24.
25 See: https://www.mindtools.com/pages/article/newLDR_83.htm
For further reading, try: R Belbin, *Management Teams: Why they Succeed or Fail* (Oxford: Butterworth-Heinemann, third edition, 2010).
26 S Cottrell, *Hit the Ground Kneeling: Seeing Leadership Differently* (London: Church House Publishing, 2012) p 3.
27 *ibid,* p 8.
28 *ibid,* p 81.
29 There are many brief introductory texts on prayer. We have used: S Cottrell, *How to Pray* (London: Church House Publishing, third edition, 2010); P Greig, *How to Pray: a Simple Guide for Normal People* (London: Hodder and Stoughton, 2019); E Pilkington, *Learning to Pray* (London: Darton, Longman and Todd, 1987); J Pritchard, *How to Pray: A Practical Handbook* (London: SPCK, 2002).
30 See for example: S Dakin and I Tarrant, *Labyrinths and Prayer Stations* (Grove Worship booklet W180); S Mainstone-Cotton, *Using Christian Contemplative Practice with Children* (London: Jessica Kingsley Publishers, 2019).
31 Mainstone-Cotton, *op cit,* p 83–84, pp 107–109.
32 Simon, *op cit,* p 9.
33 M Laird, *Into the Silent Land: the Practice of Contemplation* (London: Darton, Longman and Todd, 2006).
34 R Bristow, *Prayer in Schools* (Grove Education booklet eD11) p 3.
35 P Sheldrake, *Spirituality: A Very Short Introduction* (Oxford University Press, 2012) p 2.
36 See note 1.